MARCUS F. CAGE

WINNERS

CIRCLE

MAXIMIZE YOUR RELATIONSHIPS

PurTeaching Publishing™

Minneapolis, Minnesota 55430 USA

PurTeaching Publishing ™

Winners Circle®

Copyright© 2008

By Marcus F. Cage

WINNERS CIRCLE

MAXIMIZE YOUR RELATIONSHIPS

INTRODUCTION

The time is now for you to be blessed.

First, I would like to thank you sincerely for choosing to read this book. By taking this step you are communicating that you are ready for success. I want to let you know that this book will help you do just that, Succeed. Welcome to the *Winners Circle.*

Many people around the world desire to be the best person they can be. Unfortunately we aren't all born into the right situation for success. Therefore, smart people learn to use what they have been given and maximize it to their advantage. You must understand that everything and everyone you need is already within your reach. You can make it in life, and not just survive but you can abound.

The *Winners Circle* is a tool that can, if you work it, help you position the right people around you. This book will give you valuable insight for your relationships. I focus on the Five Levels of Relationships; *Outer Circle,*

Associate Circle, Friendship Circle, Committed Circle, and Intimate Circle. These are valuable levels that largely impact your life.

If you can learn to master these levels you can maximize your relationships. The *Winners Circle* will teach you how to take back control of your relationships and life. It delivers to you the power to complete your goals and projects by tapping into the resource of people. We will live and die by the decisions we make. If you can make better decisions in life you will have a better life. This sounds simple, but I have found that we all can use some instructions in our journey in life. God has given perfect wisdom when dealing with people; it would be wise that we listen. Thank you again and I hope that you enjoy the *Winners Circle.*

Chapter

Let's Talk "Relationships"

On occasions I have thought about my death and the legacy that I would leave for the people who have been a part of my life. I have wondered who would scramble to be a part of my send off or who would truly grieve my passing? Also, of those who knew me, which ones really knew my heart? In the end, it is my hope that those who were a part of my winners circle would celebrate my life and continue in the hope of Jesus Christ.

Every relationship you have has the potential to leave a lasting effect on people you know. I have set my heart to positively affect people around me. Whether you know it or not, relationships are key to our success in life, business and our personal pursuits. If you don't know how to utilize the relationships that you have, you run the risk of failing in life and profession. For

The Winners Circle

many years I underestimated the wonderful power of relationships. Not giving ear to its wonderfully-bitter role. Everyone has an extensive network of people whom they utilize on a day to day basis. What successful people do is identify who those people are and how they can best utilize them to benefit their purpose in life.

For some, this may sound very structured but it is equally necessary if you desire to reach your potential. I am not asking you to manipulate or con other people. Yet I am asking you to draw from the greatest resource on earth; people. Besides you must always be willing to give to those that you take from, this is a win-win situation. Only successful people and high achievers learn the lessons of how to tap into the power of relationships. What I want to bring to light in this book is this power that has been at your fingertips for most of your life. Also I would like to help you put together a winning team of people that will give you the fuel you need to do great things.

The Winners Circle

In life we know that at all times we are being used and using others. Life is largely about give and take. However when you learn how to take control over what you give, and who you give to, then true wealth can be obtained. I must explain that when I use the term wealth, success or rich, I am not necessarily referring to money. True wealth does not start externally, but internally. I have seen wealthier men and women in impoverished neighborhoods than any other place on earth. Their wealth was not measured in the amount of money in their bank account, but it rested in the value of the relationships that surrounded them.

I understand that type of thinking may be foreign to most people who grow up under this twisted western paradigm. This book will challenge some of your thinking and I hope that it will help you start building wealth in the right direction.

College is one of the most experimental times of most people's life. I knew a guy named Frank who was in an intimate

The Winners Circle

relationship with a young lady named, Ann. Ann was a pleasant person. She was mostly quiet and focused on obtaining a college degree. Frank was a handsome guy who came from a pretty good family, but he liked to flirt. He was more interested in having fun and enjoying new experiences than being tied down to one romantic relationship. Ann really fell head over heels for Frank's charming nature. They quickly became a couple. Ann was glad she found such a wonderful person who made her happy. Ann was one hundred percent invested in their relationship.

After awhile Frank flirting led to cheating. Ann was told on several occasions by her friends that he was cheating heavily, but it was hard for her to accept initially. She slowly started confronting him, but Frank would passionately deny everything. So Ann continued to invest into what she thought was an exclusively intimate relationship leading to marriage. Frank on the other hand, had feelings for Ann, but they were mostly feelings of pity and obligation. He wasn't mature enough to tell her that she was just a pit stop on his journey and not his destination.

Things continued to get worse for the couple until finally Ann caught Frank with another young lady. She was shocked and appalled at what she witnessed. A large part of her heart died that day. She dropped out of college and moved back home with her parents. Frank tried to apologize but in a way he was relieved that it happened that way. Besides he really wanted to move on to other adventures.

Unfortunately, this type of relationship experience happens in our society more than people think. Relationships are very powerful and should not be under estimated. They can be used to push a person into greatness or they can be abused to steal the soul of great people. Ann was doomed from the beginning. She let a wolf into her intimate circle and even when she was warned who he really was, she didn't have the fortitude to put him out.

The Winners Circle

I know that most of you reading this book have had similar if not some of the same situations happen to you or people you know. Ann's whole life and future changed from one relationship. Some people love hard. Some people give one hundred and one percent of who they are into their relationships. They don't hold back anything and they risk it all. This book is really for you. All of you who dive in heart first and don't look back, I want to help you "guard your heart and true treasure."

We live in a society that preaches individuality more than any culture that exist on this earth. However, every successful person that have reached the height of their profession or calling never did it alone. The truth is that it takes more than one person to become successful. Rather you know it or not we all can use an *entourage.* It can be your family or a combination of friends, family, and associates. If you want to reach your potential it will take a group of people that are committed to helping you reach your potential and becoming successful at what you do.

The truth is you're the answer and solution that you have been looking for. You are gifted to do great and wonderful things in your life time. Your winners circle is only there to multiply your gifts and talents in ways that you never thought possible. What you must understand is that, true power is not in money it is in people. Anyone who chases money has already lost in life. Many people make it their purpose to gain more money, but in the process they lose valuable relationships that will never be replaced. That isn't a good gamble; always choose valuable people over money. If you can't salvage a relationship or two, you are doomed to be alone and lonely as you suck in the thin air at the top of the money mountain.

It is naive for us to look from the outside-in and think that successful people reach the heights of their success alone. This is a grave misconception. I have been

The Winners Circle

the pastor at Refuge Christian Center for five years. It wasn't until the second year of ministering that God revealed to me the secret of how to reach my potential and achieve great success. He told me that I could not do it alone and no one was going to show up on a white horse to save me from my agony. In fact, I would have to go out by inspiration of the Holy Spirit and build a team of people that would later become my "Winners Circle."

This group of people would play key roles in my success. After many months of prayer I began to seek out men and women that would provide different needs, Christian and non-Christian. You may say that this system is a little selfish but you must understand that being a *little* selfish is a part of a healthy life. Those of us that are in the caring business we sometime get caught up with caring for others instead of saving a little something for ourselves. The *Winners Circle* will help you put the necessary people around you that will care for you and push you into a wealthier lifestyle.

The Winners Circle

Let's Talk "Relationships"

Help!!! I'm being used.

You should not enter into a relationship with the fear of being used. It is absurd; you are being used every day of your life. This idea is a simple relationship delusion. It's funny when I hear someone say she is being used by someone she is in a relationship. Hello, that's what relationships are about.

I'm not talking about being manipulated or abused. If you live, play, and work around people, let me share a little secret with you; you are being used and not always getting a return on your charity. You are being used to some degree by the little old lady whom you open the door for.

> *Those of us that are in the caring business we sometime get caught up with caring for others instead of saving a little something for ourselves.*

The Winners Circle

You are being used by family and friends who never pay you back the money they owe you. Also there are those mutual occasions where you may have some benefit such as, an invite to a wedding, church or event. The event may not be a main interest for you, but you attend anyway. You are still being used. I believe that we were made to be a resource for other people, especially, those people who walk in love and understand agape love. Besides, every person that practice agape love has favor and reaps a continually bountiful harvest from the Lord and other people.

The greatest relationships are those that exercise *Agape*. The state of agape is when love is given unconditionally to someone. I must tell you that you don't arrive at this point easily. It is something that you must practice, practice, and practice. I'll be frank, many of the relationships Christians or non-Christians have will never *stay* at this level. You might ask the question, "Why should I try to reach for something I can't have? I never said that you can't have it, but I will tell you that it cannot be maintained by any human for a great length of time. Agape is a divine quality. Consider 1 Corinthians 13:4-8;

> *4 Love suffers long, and is kind; love envies not; love vaunts not itself, is not puffed up, 5 Does not behave itself rudely, seeks not her own, is not easily provoked, keeps no record of evil; 6 Rejoices not in iniquity, but rejoices in the truth; 7 Bears all things, believes all things, hopes all things, endures all things. 8 Love never fails...*

I have been married eleven years. In that time I have slowly learned to sacrifice my personal wants for the greater benefit of my family. This is what it means to die daily. Not because I wanted to but because the relationship demanded me to. That may sound bad to you, but death of personal *want* is sometimes necessary within the marriage relationship, such as hanging out with the fellows 3-4 nights a week. After reading 1 Corinthians 13:4-8 over and over, through the years, it still seems impossible. You may even understand what love requires, but to carry it out is another ball game. It's only possible through learning Christ.

> *I believe that we were made to be a resource for other people, especially, those people who walk in love and understand agape love.*

You tell me who wants to suffer in a relationship? No one signs up for suffering, especially by the hand of the one with whom you are in the relationship. The first statement in the scripture contradicts the current American teaching on relationships. Media promotes that your relationships are the source of your happiness. If you are not happy, whether it is with a marriage or friend relationship, you should dispose of it and get a new one. This teaching has flooded the culture of Christian relationships. Suffering of some degree is a part of life and relationships. In most cases, it makes the individual stronger as well as the relationship. However, relationships must have boundaries. Christ teaches us to prayerfully consider dissolving a relationship when the three A's occur; abuse, abandonment, and adultery.

There are still those cases where some suffering is necessary but not desired. What if your spouse found out that he/she has cancer and the doctor informs you that the next year will be the hardest thing your relationship has experienced? Is it time to leave? For the next year your relationship will suffer great trauma. It will not be the happy times that you signed up for. Your spouse may lose hair, breast(s), or the ability to procreate. Their mood and personality will change drastically. This is real life.

Sometimes in life, tribulations help you find out who you really are, as well as those who are around you. This truth may be difficult for a lot of people to accept. In fact, a lot of people will and have walked away from relationships they feared may cause them any degree of suffering. There is a way to handle relationships of all kind and the burdens they carry. The following chapters of this book will reveal this timeless knowledge.

Chapter

Emotional Banking

Your emotion bank is a result of your *winners circle*. The people around you are responsible for making frequent deposits that positively feed and strengthen your emotional integrity. Your emotions are like a lake and your feelings flow from it. If your emotional bank is weak you will find yourself offended easily and frustrated frequently by those around you.

Think about it. Every person you hold a relationship with has an emotional price. This price is what you pay when you engage and

Suffering of some degree is a part of life and relationships.

interact with them on a daily basis. Some people, fortunately, put back some of what they take, but that isn't always the case.

Emotional Banking

I had an associate who was homeless. Periodically, I would take him to a restaurant to eat. At the beginning of our time hanging out it would usually start off good, but every once and awhile we would get into an occasional confrontation. However, that didn't bother me much. I never really fed into his games. It was when we went to a restaurant that he withdrew loads of emotional currency from my bank.

Without fail, he would have an issue with the waiter or his order. It was bad. There were times that he would want to go back to the chef and ask him/her to make him a special dish. I was so embarrassed. On one occasion he made this huge scene because he felt his meal didn't have enough onions. I couldn't believe it. It made me so upset that I paid for the meal and walked out to my car.

He stayed in the restaurant and got his doggy bag before he joined me. I found that after leaving him I felt very drained and vexed. It felt like someone had beaten my emotions with a sledge hammer. It would take months sometimes before I could hang out with him again. He was the type of person who would withdraw more then I wanted him too.

You also have those types of people in your life. They take, take, take but they don't give anything back. The truth is, you can't have too many people within your circle like this. Your *winners circle* should be made up of people who deposit into your life more then they withdraw. Now, your circle will have some people that withdraw from your bank, but within your overall circle you must come out ahead. This makes a healthy circle of relationships.

You should learn who withdraws, deposits, and who does both. There should be people who give you the charge you need to make it through the day or week. You should be able to tap into someone's anointing at all times. When you really get advanced you will learn exactly what each person gives or takes. There is a scripture in the Bible that states, "Men will give into your bosom" (*Luke 6:38KJ*).   When you have a healthy and steady circle of relationships you can take on more challenging people, and projects.   However if you don't have enough people who are depositing into your life, you need to stay away from these people who tend to withdraw too much emotionally from you too fast.

I'm big on lists.   I believe that it is good to see what your thoughts look like in written form.   So at this point I would like you to write down the people within your *winners circle* and what they do; deposit, withdraw or both.

~Next Page~

Your Emotional Bank

DEPOSIT	WITHDRAW	BOTH
Bobby S.	*Cathy P.*	*Dan B.*
1.		
2.		
3.		
4.		
5.		
6.		
7.		
8.		
9.		
10.		

Now you have an idea of what your true circle look like. Remember, honesty is the key in this exercise. Don't give someone credit for *both* if they take more then they give, in the end they may be a taker anyway. However, I will advise you to think about the big picture. Factor in what they are like normally. For example, a person could be a steady depositor, but what if they start going through some personal hardships such as, divorce, illness or job lost. Think carefully, you don't want to distance yourself just because someone in your circle is going through a season of hardship. It is the continual withdrawers that you want to watch out for. They don't need a season they always have issues. After you have an idea of what you are working with, now it's time to make some life changing decisions.

> *Your Winners Circle should be made up of people who deposit into your life more then they withdraw.*

At the beginning of building your *winners circle* you shouldn't have any withdrawers. After you have built a stronger circle of relationships, you may be able to take on more challenging people. If you do have people who are withdrawing (with the exception of family members, this will be discussed more in chapter 11) you need to relocate them ASAP to your *outer-circle*. As we build your winners circle you will learn how to effectively relocate people from space to space. However, at this time, as a part of the first step in removing them, you need to cross out the names of the people on your list who fall under the "withdraw" column. Don't just X out the whole column, but go through and cross each person off individually.

Example: ~~Michael L. – Withdraw~~

I know this may seem hard for you but you are not completely stopping your relationship with that person. You will learn how to relate differently with him/her. One of the biggest pitfalls you must watch out for at this point is *soul-ties.* There are people within your circle of relationships who aren't really good for you *now*, but you have become *soul-tied* to them. While you feel that strong connection and even some obligation to the person it is nevertheless a bad or negative connection. It must be broken so that you can reach you potential.

There was a person I had formed a soul-tie with for about two years. I thought I was helping her but she was acting as an anchor to me. I learned the hard way that these people can stop your progress, and the only way to move forward is to cut the connection and reposition them.

When you have repositioned the main withdrawers within your relationship circle, you will be ready to move to the next level within your *winners circle*. The next part of the winners circle will help you arrange the people you have listed into five circles or spaces of relationships. Let me give you a valuable piece of information. Some of your old relationships may not be able to help you get to where you are going. So if at the end of this arrangement you feel you are in unfamiliar waters, you are, but don't be afraid. You will build by prayer and patience a *winners circle* that will become the most valuable asset in your life.

Chapter

Dealing with Relationship Pain

Unfortunately, pain and suffering is a part of life that no one can escape. Pain doesn't discriminate. It crosses race barriers, and every class of people all over the world can identify with its sting. The average person will experience more pain and suffering through relationships than any other source in their life. Many things cause pain for many different people. However, my pain triggers could be different than your pain triggers.

So, I have to ask the question: why so much pain in relationships? Is there a divine reason for this phenomenon?

> *It is the continual withdrawers that you want to watch out for.*

Can we use it to our advantage? Well, to get the answers to such eternal questions, I had to turn to the only eternal God I know: Jesus Christ.

Let's take a look at the affects of pain for a minute. When *pain* is applied to the body from external objects, the mind quickly defends the body by escaping the pain. For example, if your hand accidentally touches a hot pot, your mind would immediately withdraw your hand away. There would be an instant reaction without much thought. Also, you would be more careful in the future when you are around hot pots. This is what I like to call *general pain*. This isn't pain or suffering that God intends for us to necessarily experience, but it just occurs as every person blunders through their life. Through our general pain, we learn our environmental and personal limitations. They can be identified by *external scars* on your body. We all have scars on our body that show the valuable lessons we have learned while growing up.

There is a second kind of pain that is more than skin deep. I call it *special pain*. It affects your emotions, feelings, ego, and identity. Unlike general pain, special pain is more internalized. The scars it leaves you with can be temporarily hidden or masked from people you know. Therefore, it can be more dangerous to you because things that can be hidden in dark places are less likely to be healed.

If thy whole body therefore be full of light, having no part dark, the whole shall be full of light, as when the bright shining of a candle doth give thee light. (Luke 11: 36)KJ

The simple affects of *special pain* are the same as general pain, they both hurt. Yet the reaction time to special pain can be slower. For example, if a young lady experience emotionally hurt and pain in her first romantic relationship with a young man, she will eventually withdraw from him. Her emotions, feelings, ego, and identity will send her mind the message that she needs to withdraw from the pain he caused if she wants to remain healthy.

This is how general and special pain is different. When special pain occurs, there can be some delay in how quick a person withdraws from the one causing them pain. This reaction depends on individual healthiness. A healthy individual will be more cautious in their future relationships with other people. However, one bad experience may not drastically affect her next relationship. If she continues to experience special pain as result of, cheating, lying, rape or molestation, it can completely sever her ability to properly receive and give love.

Special pain has the potential to completely destroy your *relationship bridges*. These draw bridges are very important within your winners circle. You need to know when you should or should not extend your bridge to others. There are other types of bridges such as, communication, understanding, patience and intimacy, but the most important one is your trust bridge.

Trust is vital in all types of relationships. When your trust bridge has been severely abused it doesn't easily extend to anyone. In fact, a lot of people are walking around today with serious bridge damage. It's not sensible to continue extending your trust bridge and not allowing it time to heal. You must allow healing to take place in your heart before extending it to others. When you decide to finally extend your trust bridge, the new person must be patient and walk very carefully because your trust bridge may still be a little weak. It will need some reinforcements to keep it strong. When trust is strong within your relationship it gives you an amazingly firm pedestal to develop from.

When pain isn't managed properly, it can cause serious *traffic jams* within the inner person. A person might desire to move forward in new relationships but because pervious pain wasn't managed and healed properly, the new relationship is doomed to be stuck in relationship traffic.

Pain is real and the smarter you become at managing it, the better your winners circle will become. God has released healing for the scars that we all carry. It doesn't matter how dark or hidden it is, God has the ability to love your pain away.

> *It's not sensible to continue extending your trust bridge and not allowing it time to heal.*

Now there is a positive side to pain that I must admit. If pain is managed correctly, it can be the fuel that pushes you into greater success. The reality is that we can't stop the pain that life hands out, but we can use it for our benefit. The positive aspect of pain is seldom realized and therefore seldom utilized.

Growing up, I used to believe that there was a force trying to stop me from becoming successful because of all the pain I experienced from family, friends, and society. Now, I have learned there is a force, but it can't stop me. I know how to take the pain and turn it into fuel/motivation. Every time I think about quitting or throwing in the towel, I simply say, "No". I can't, and you can't let the enemy win. He can't stop you or anything that God has placed in your hands. The enemy is a liar and a murderer. You are more than a conqueror through Christ Jesus that strengthens you. So even though the pain and hurt of this life is great at times, you must learn how to harness the hurt, take the pain and achieve a greater success.

The reality is that we all can have success and the best that life has to offer. However, the greatest thing that will stand in the way of you achieving your goals is how you manage the pain, hurt, and the daily stressors of life. The winners circle is your key to unlocking power that has been with you all alone.

Chapter

Whose Fault is it Anyway?

As I said before, every relationship suffers trauma and tribulation. However some trails are not the fault of either partner. These troubles exist within every relationship. I like to call them *no-fault circumstances*. Every relationship will have its share of these *no-fault circumstances*. In these conflicts, no one is directly to blame for the troubles that occur. For example, if your child is diagnosed as autistic or bipolar it's not the parents fault, it's a *no-fault circumstance*.

After being married for eleven years there are still some things that I do that upset my wife. I don't intentionally desire to upset her, but our differences have a tendency of causing conflict from time to time. For example, I don't always put my dirty clothes in the laundry basket. I have a tendency of leaving them everywhere around the house. My wife and I have had heated conversations about why I can't simply put my clothes where they suppose to go. My answer is, "I will do better next time honey." Actually, I do follow through for about a week or so but eventually I go back to my old way of doing things. I don't mean her any harm. I really have tried to change, and I have gotten better over time. Yet there are still times where my dysfunctional way of doing things come to the surface. She knows now that I'm not intentionally trying to upset her. It is a *no-fault circumstance.*

> *When your trust bridge has been severely abused it doesn't easily extend to anyone.*

Now, there is another circumstance that is more threatening to your relationships that I like to call, *my-fault circumstance.* These circumstances are the result of intentional mischievous behavior of someone within the relationship. *My-fault circumstances* can be more difficult for the victim to find the intent-of-action. This makes them very difficult to resolve. They can be forgiven but sometimes they are not resolved. Fact is, we create more trouble for ourselves than life or the enemy could ever give us. It's true that most of us may have overall good intentions, but the ability to carry out those intention are far from us. We hurt one another; it's sad, but true.

Your intent-of-action is your *only witness* of your true intent toward those you are in a relationship with. The problem with your true intent is that it can't openly testify to those you are in relationships with. Sure you can tell a person you didn't mean to hurt them, but how will they truly know? So most of the time people take as much trouble and tribulation as they can from one another, and when they *feel* they are being used or manipulated, they start pushing people away. Reacting this way isn't bad but there are some circumstances that call for you to stick in there and see things through.

The exception to this is abuse, abandonment and adultery.

Running usually sounds like a good way to preserve self and protect your *emotional bank*, but let me share a story with you. There was a woman that was truly wounded from her childhood. She suffered rap, maltreatment, abuse, molestation, and she never had a healthy male in her life that wanted anything more than a sexual experience from her. As she aged, she found that there weren't many doors of opportunity opening for her so she accepted the only one that was open. When she had hit hard times the only door she felt could help her out of an economic decline was stripping for money.

She justified it in her head as a temporary fix and not something she planned to do long term. However, after many years she had graduated to all out prostitution. Deep within her heart she knew she was meant to be more than a sex object. At one time in her life she had dreams and better desires, but she had locked them away in her heart because survival at some point became her number one priority.

One day she met a man that treated her different than any other man she had ever experienced. He even went as far as to tell her that he was sent by God to save her life and give her the honor that had eluded her all of her life. She was scared and amazed at his genuineness. Still afraid and amazed she said yes to his lofty ideas. In three years time she was the proud mother of two beautiful children and had the honor of a new fellowship of friends and associates. He had given her a quiet peaceful life and the freedom to unlock the doors of her dreams and desires.

In the fourth year she somehow became bored with peace and tranquility. She missed something about her old person. She frequently allowed her mind to walk backwards and explore the different men and places she had experienced in the past.

Whose Fault is it Anyway?

After awhile contempt for her new life had set in her heart. She began lightly flirting with men and before long she had given herself to infidelity.

> *After being married for eleven years there are still something's that I do that upset my wife. I don't intentionally desire to upset her, but our differences have a tendency of causing conflict from time to*

What's sad is that she continued to cheat on her husband and family. The only thing different about her return to her old life the second time around was that she wasn't doing it for money anymore. She knew in her heart that it didn't make since that she had returned to her lovers but she somehow felt more familiar with that environment.

Her husband found out about her lustful affairs. He was completely hurt.

However he was reminded that her current choices fit her old lifestyle. He learned that she had never let her promiscuous nature die. You might say that this is too farfetched, and not even close to a real life experience. No one would ever do that. Unfortunately, this story is true. It is the story of the prophet Hosea and his wife Gomer.

God used this experience to show Hosea what it was like to love Israel, and how she played the Harlot even after He had given her honor and blessings. What's important for you to know is that true love may suffer greatly within its relationships. However, I wouldn't want you or anyone to experience what Hosea went through. The point here is that some relationships within your circle may be there to humble you. People will be at fault, but be careful and prayerful about each relationship you have.

Truth is, relationships that you exercise love in are the most humbling. What's funny about being humbled is that it is closely related to being humiliated. It's for this reason that most people would rather not fully commit their love within relationships. Fear of being humiliated and being used are two walls that people put up which stops them from truly galvanizing with the person they are trying to relate to.

Oh, and by the way, everyone is being used in some way. Though you can't control rather or not you are used, you can control how and by whom you are used. Learning to be more careful in your relationships is what the winners circle is all about.

Chapter

Take A Hard Look Into Your Past

There are some parts of my life while growing up that I could totally erase out of my memory. Don't get me wrong, my entire past wasn't all bad it's just certain parts of my past that to this day, I have problems dealing with. You may be able to agree. This has led me to ask some questions. Why is our past so important? Does it affect us as adults? Can it negatively affect our ability to have future healthy relationships? Can your past experiences stop you from having a successful marriage? Can your past stop you from believing and trusting in the Lord?

These are some of the questions this chapter will help you explore. It is very important to know your past and how it has shaped you good or bad. You should at least be honest about your experiences. You don't have to dwell on things but at least be aware.

Take A Hard Look at your Past

I wasn't born with a golden spoon in my mouth. In fact, life in Mississippi was at times more bitter than sweet. However, I'm not embarrassed of that fact. My past is a part of who I am today. I love who I am and where I come from and so should you.

> *Truth is, relationships that you exercise love in are the most humbling.*

We all have to live with ourselves. Therefore, why not deal with who you really are? Your past holds a large part of who you are or used to be. This is why people will move thousands of miles away from their home town, trying to forget who they once were and where they came from. The reality is that, we all have monsters great and small, in our closets. So we must deal with them and move forward in life.

I want to tell you this, before you go any further in this book. Your past isn't unforgivable. It can be covered by the grace of Jesus Christ. He knows you inside and out. He knows every mistake and every short coming. He understands all the suffering you have experienced. He knows every mask you wear. Jesus will help you bring all dark things to light. Why not face the truth and be healed? If you don't receive healing from your past hurt and pain, the process of building a *winners circle* will be extremely difficult for you. The *winners circle* will demand that you trust certain people, but if you have trust issues related to authority figures, you will have a hard time listening to mentors and associates that can give valuable advice.

As a child I really thought I was ugly and unattractive. I had a serious pimple problem. It seemed like my face was covered with pimples all the time. It was as if every inch of my face had some kind of bump on it, well it felt like it. On top of that, I had a very unattractive scar on the side of my mouth left from an accident as a kid. It made all my smiles look a little uneven.

When picture day at school came, I would try to make some lame excuse to get out of taking it. I can remember just staring at other kid's and desiring to have a nice mouth or smooth face. You want to talk about low self-esteem. I was the poster child for low self-esteem. Yet these were things I could not talk about, much less put in a book.

Now, if that wasn't enough, my mother wasn't able to afford the latest fashions or hottest gear. So, I had a little drawer full of hand-me-downs and out of date trends. Of course this caused me to become a loner. I remember as a child looking in the mirror, wishing I could change into someone different.

I believe that most people may have had some of the same or similar issues I did with low self-esteem. If you were like me, you spent a lot of time asking God why me? Well, today God will answer you.

*For I reckon that the **sufferings** of this present time are **not worthy** to be compared with the glory which shall be **revealed in us**. For the earnest expectation of the creature waits for the manifestation of the sons of God. For **the creature was made subject to vanity**, **not willingly**, but by reason of him who has subjected the same in hope, Because the creature itself also shall be delivered from the bondage of corruption into the glorious liberty of the children of God. (Romans 8: 18-21)KJ*

The truth is we all experience storms, showers, and trials throughout our lives. It's what every human being has in common. It can come in different forms and fashions but it's just some type of storm you must make it through. We all experience some type of special pain or general pain. Special pain and hurt may stay with us all our lives. Children are molested, raped, abused, exposed to all types of horror, and neglected everyday in America. Why does God let this happen? Why can't God put children in beautiful homes and give them two kind and loving parents who will care for them?

Well, here is the hard truth. God is fair, but the world isn't. I know some of you may not fully agree but let's dive into it a little deeper. A child is basically the product of two people. The parents can either be *cursed or blessed.* God respects the decisions of every person and gives them the right to choose. He forces no one to choose Him. Also, the Lord gives them the fruit of their choices. Therefore, a child can be born into a cursed or blessed household. The household that the child is born into may be chosen by God, but He doesn't have a vendetta against anyone. In fact, your parents choose what type of household environment and atmosphere their child will be raised in. So if your early childhood was bad, don't blame God, He had to honor the choices of your parents.

Take A Hard Look at your Past

I call heaven and earth to record this day **against you**, *that I have set before you* **life and death, blessing and cursing**: *therefore* **choose life**, *that* **both you and your seed may live**. *(Deuteronomy 30:19)KJ.*

If you don't receive healing from your past hurt and pain this process of building a winners circle will be extremely difficult for you.

Please Stop Blaming God For Your Past

Every human being is attached to the choices and decisions of their parents. God begs us to choose life. If your father and mother were drunkards, abusers, and ignorant, then that's the environment that you were raised in.

Even though the conditions of your birth and childhood could have been undesirable, remember **you** have an advocate in the Father. The Bible teaches that *"...the* **sufferings** *of this present time are* **not worthy** *to be compared with the glory which shall be* **revealed in us"** *(Romans 8:18).KJ*

Before your sufferings were past-tense, they were present at the time of inflection. This is to say that the pain and suffering of your past can not compare to the possibility of success in your future. *Don't let your past burn your bridges of future possibilities.*

Your parents may have made the wrong choices, and reaped a hellish environment. You may not know the presence of God and the peace that passes all understanding. However, God didn't let that environment kill you. You may have gone through *some* of the curse, but God was waiting in the wings for His opportunity to offer *you life and that much more abundantly.* It is God's hope that the special pain that you experienced hasn't *blinded your ability to make the right decision.* He knows that the blessings that He will share with you are more than any struggle that you have suffered in your past. In fact, the deeper the pain inflected on you, the more glorious the gift He will share with you. If only you would choose different than your parents. If you are obedient to His word and way He will help you *forgive whate*ver happened.

God can make up for the curse that was on your household. God is fair. Jesus is more than the curse, but you must choose Him, and see that He is God. The word of God teaches, *"For the creature (you) was made subject to vanity (the curse), not willingly (not your fault)" (Romans 8:20)KJ*. God knows the situation better than you think. Jesus has reached out to you from the cross and offered you the cure to past hurt and pain. Our Lord knows that you were at the mercy of those that were without his counsel or guidance. What you have to come to realize now is that without God, things will never work out. You have a choice. Choose life in Christ and live again.

Our past has a way of never dying. It can sometimes be a sore that gets worse and worse as life goes on, if you let it. Don't let the scars of your past hurt and pain prevent you from being successful. Dysfunctional behavior that you may have learned while in your youth can become a stronghold and a stumbling block, stopping your forward progress.

Like you, I was exposed to many evils and ungodly things while growing up. For example, the volume in my household was always set on *loud*. This didn't make for a peaceful space. My family would express happiness and anger almost at the same volume and tone. It was confusing at first, but after awhile I learned to adapt. I came to understand that if I wanted to be heard, I had better get loud. This was my way of adapting to my environment. However, this had a negative effect on my interpersonal relationships, and other areas of my life as a young African American male.

"Loud," became the way that I solved problems, and communicated in life. In my relationships, I felt that I had to raise my voice to be truly heard. It wasn't that I wanted to fight, but it was just my way of communicating. When it came to me expressing myself, I would get all wide-eyed and boisterous or be completely withdrawn. I would use large intense arm movements to tell my side of the story. That may have worked if I was in the streets, but everyone couldn't understand that style of communicating. So a lot of my problems in relationships went unresolved because all that was heard was confusion and fear.

Instead of communicating with love, I was communicating with intimidation. The crazy part was that I thought this behavior was normal for everyone. I felt that I just had more passion about my point of view. However, it was and is a somewhat threatening form of communication. People stop listening when your volume gets too highly aggressive.

Unfortunately I didn't know any better, it was the only way I was taught. It's how my people in my environment taught me to communicate. The problem was, and still is, that way might help you survive on the street, but it will definitely hurt you within your relationships, jobs, and other environments.

Even though it was causing pain and stress in my life and to others, I didn't want to let go of that part of me. I had lived with it all my life. I felt I would be selling out, or something along those lines. Little did I know, throwing off that weight would help me float better in the sea of life. It was, in fact, slowing me down, causing me to sink. I was blind to the real truth of what it takes to truly be prosperous.

I've heard people say things like, "this is who I am, take it or leave it." What they don't understand is that their past is about to hold them back from their future. Some change must be embraced if you are going to have any chance at a prosperous life. Every great person experiences their own evolution. If you don't evolve, you become extinct and die off.

If you were trained and given the tools in your past to survive the streets, what happens when you're no longer on the streets? Do you act the same way in the white collar world or do you deny that there is a white collar world? It's a different set of rules. How do you survive and succeed in it? You wouldn't bring shoulder pads and a helmet to a baseball game. People would laugh you off the field.

There is no way you could be successful at baseball with that type of attitude and equipment. You might love football, but when it's time to play baseball, take off the gear and suit up for the game. People with loud, boisterous ways of communication come off as threatening. It's about changing hats or simply switching from an outside voice to an inside voice.

*Therefore if any man be in Christ, he is a **new creature: old things are passed away;** behold, **all things are become new.** (2 Corinthians 5:17)KJ*

If you intend on having God in your life, believe me, He is about to change some things about your character. Every part of you that don't emulate Him will be challenged to change. That's if you desire success in life. It took me many years to realize that I had to change the way I communicated in different situations.

God designed us to be successful at life. I know that the famous term "sell out" has been dubbed as a negative description. However, this is exactly what has to happen. We must sell-out every past behavior that stops us from transforming into the image of God.

Think about this. If you were dropped in the middle of China with nothing but the clothes on your back, what would you have to do to get your needs met? You would have to learn the language and culture. You would have to learn how to communicate to those who had the power to meet your needs. That's if you like to eat. It wouldn't mean that you would be selling out your race or culture or forgetting where you come from. You don't stop being an American because you learned how to speak Chinese. In fact, what it means is that you have increased your capacity and value. You have moved forward. Change is the catalyst to prosperity.

> For **though I be free** from all men, yet have I **made myself servant to all**, **that I might gain** the more (successful at what I do). And to the Jews I became as a Jew, that I might gain the Jews... To them that are without law, as without law... that I might gain them that are without law. **To the weak became I as weak,** that I might gain the weak: **I am made all things to all men**, that I might by all means save some. (1 Corinthians 9:19-22)KJ

This is a powerful group of scripture. This speaks to Paul's ability to adapt and complete his assignment in any environment that he was in. He didn't feel like he was losing himself or selling out. In fact, he felt like he was gaining. Paul had made up his mind that in order for him to communicate the Gospel to others in different situation and environments, he would have to change his way of communicating and relating.

I moved to Minnesota from Mississippi in 1987. Minnesota is a completely opposite state from Mississippi. At that time, it wasn't cool to be from the south or have a thick southern accent. In high school, kids would find it absolutely amusing to hear me talk. Of course that caused me to shut down and withdraw from the popular crowds.

> *Some change must be embraced if you are going to have any chance at a prosperous life. Every great person experiences their own evolution. If you don't evolve, you become extinct and die off.*

One day in the tenth grade when I was at a basketball practice, I told my coach that I was tired. In fact, I said, "I'm tied, Coach". He thought I said "I's tied, coach," like a slave or something. He and the entire team fell down laughing at my expense.

I played along and laughed at the incident, but I was deeply hurt. I knew at that point that I had to learn how to communicate as a Minnesotan. I never felt that I was selling out my Mississippi roots. I am thankful of where I come from. However, where I am and where God is taking me is more important.

Don't let the pain of your past paralyze your ability to take hold of the future God has in store for you. God desires you to have *good success.* Your past may not have been the best. In fact, it may have been downright crazy but you can have a different future. Jesus tells you to "Come to him and He will give us rest." *(Matthew 11:228)KJ.* Your healing depends on your ability to forgive all them who hurt you in your past and caused you pain. Forgiveness is a powerful weapon in the fight against the enemy. If you can't forgive those who hurt you, then how can God forgive you the pain you caused and are causing others? The more forgiveness you give, the more forgiveness you receive. You can be set free and *"Whom the Son set free is free indeed."(John 8:36)KJ*

I know most of you may have wanted some complex answer. However, don't get happy just yet. You might have to call a few people to tell them that you forgive them for what they did to you in the past. This is a powerful piece in the process of your healing. By releasing them, you will be releasing yourself.

For if ye forgive men their trespasses, your heavenly Father will also forgive you. But if ye forgive not men their trespasses, neither will your Father forgive your trespasses. (Matthew 6:14-15)KJ

By not forgiving the people that hurt you in your past, you allow them to hurt you every day afterward. If you don't get this right, you will perpetuate the same past hurt to those that are a part of your *winners circle.* Jesus teaches the believer how to be set free from the bondage of their past hurt.

An old friend of mine confessed to me that she had been molested when she was a child by a family member. She said that for many years the thoughts of the event tormented her, even into her adulthood. She could not believe that this person who should have been protecting her was in fact preying on her as a little girl.

After she was older, she would dread his presence at her yearly family events and holidays. In fact, she said that she would always try to keep her distance from him. In the future, her past hurt spilled over into her ability to trust other men she had relationships with.

It wasn't until she actually had a child that she had the strength to privately confront the family member. Truth was, she was afraid for her child's safety with him around. She wasn't willing to stop visiting family events so she had to make a decision to talk to him. After confronting him about the past events, she said that it felt like a weight was lifted off her shoulders. She had given back the uneasiness that she felt so many times before to its owner. Later she was able to have healthier relationships.

> *Don't let the pain of your past paralyze your ability to take hold of the future God has in store for you*

Finally, I must say that the past has passed. I do understand that some people don't like to dig up old memories, but when those memories are harming your life in the present, you must deal with them. By taking a hard look at your past, you may discover answers you have been looking for.

Preparing to Relate To Others

Many times in everyday relationships, people reach a point of no return. At this point they may say something like "I can't take this anymore". This doesn't just happen in romantic relationships, but it's possible in almost every relationship you may have. When people feel that they are giving and not receiving or being out right taken advantage of, they want to find better relationships.

The subject of relationships is ageless. Most people believe that they are experts at relationships simply because they know how to manipulate people and use people to get what they want. However, that is not how we are supposed to use relationships. It is one of the most fundamentally common networks that everyone access on a daily basis. However, few people know how to utilize their relationship circles properly. If you take the time to learn how to manage your relationships, you will learn how to reach your potential in life. When you get the right people around you, they can be the fuel you need to do great things.

Unfortunately, relationships are not taught in high school. If I had my way, every high school would offer relationship classes. Life cruelly teaches most people how to relate to one another. When a child starts school, they move outside of their family sphere of influence. Unconsciously, they slowly start exercising what has been modeled in their immediate family. If you have been given a descent family model, the chances of you managing your relationships well are descent. However, most people today don't have descent family models. The dysfunctional family is the normal. Therefore, most people chances of relating well toward others are slim to no chance. Even when intentions are good, people still don't know *how* to live out their love toward one another.

Preparing to Relate To Others

When you don't know how to use relationships properly you will abuse the relationships you have. For example, when a man doesn't know nor understand what the purpose of a woman is, he will manipulate, and abuse her natural purpose. He may even have deep regard for her but without modeling, mentoring, parenting, and accountability, he will relate to her from a selfish core.

So let's define this thing called relationship? Relationships are simply the degree of connectivity that you have and maintain with a person, place or thing. It is how we relate to our environment, to people, to animals, to the earth, to God and every other significant noun in our life.

We have all been directly affected by relationships, starting with our immediate and extended family. The relationships that you have seen modeled before you usually set the tone for how you relate to others that you encounter and engage with. If you did not grow up with good role models, it will make your relationships hard and full of disappointment or heartache.

Most of the time there are more misses than hits. Too many misses or bad relationships can quickly lead to a bitter and hard heart. I believe that when we realize and identify our own flaws and dysfunctions then we can *learn* how to develop our ability to relate to others.

Anyone can master the ability to genuinely relate to other people. You must understand that as our world becomes more and more populated, isolation will not be a possibility. Your *winners circle* will help you take the *power of relationship* back. You don't have to be perfect in how you relate but you will have to learn some basic tools of dealing with people.

Your network of relationships is so important that you will either flourish or slowly decline by the way you form and maintain them. Your ability to create a sound network of people will prove your ability to relate in this world. I believe that everyone can learn how to relate to those who are around them. To be honest, this is not rocket science. This book will help you build a solid foundation of valuable relationships that will help you become the person you've always desired to be. Though I can teach you many principles, you must take the time to practice what is taught.

Chapter

Identify Your Current Circle

The weird thing about people is that they choose some of the worst people to be a part of their relationship circle. Afterwards they wonder, "Why isn't my life smoother?" I have found that some people don't really have the strength of character to keep dangerous people out of their relationship circles. In life, we must choose our friends carefully.

Choosing the right relationships for your winners circle is more about safety than anything else. If you think that you are valuable and have at least some self-worth then it would be wise to protect yourself from wolves and foxes. Keeping yourself safe is a necessary part of living a healthy life.

You owe it to yourself and your family to be cautious about who comes in and out your life. At times you must know that it is okay to rearrange and relocate people who don't respect the position they occupy within your inner circle. We are going to identify relationship *assets and liabilities* that exist within your life today.

When I first did this, I realized that there were a couple of people in my life who had to be relocated. It wasn't that I didn't love them, but it was that they did not respect the space they occupied in my life. It was a *no-fault-situation*. There was a difference of vision and values that had taken place but we had never taken the time to identify our differences. I know this may all sound like a very structured process, but it is the most valuable assessment you can do for yourself and others. After doing it for awhile, you will get the hang of it quickly.

If you can commit to doing the work in the beginning of your relationships, it makes everything else easier. But because most people relate with great levels of dysfunction, they normalize even the most abusive and hurtful relationships. It is in your best interest to watch the people that you *have* to have some level of relationship with. The Bible teaches, "...know them which labor among you..."*(1 Thess 5:12)KJ*

Even the average person exists within an enormous web of relationships. Unfortunately, most people don't really have an effective system of navigating relationships successfully. It's not until that long anticipated crisis or knock-out drag-out argument or fight finally occur when someone really hurts you that you realize that your system sucks.

I don't believe that you don't know the people within your relationship network. Most people casually know about their relationship circle but they haven't organized them. You could say its intuition, discernment, instinct, insight, but we know beyond words if someone suits us. Though you can't be with everyone 24/7, there is a spiritual connection that gives you great insight to those that you share your time with. If you learn how to operate in the spiritual connection of your relationships, it will help guide you pass the manipulative words that negative people use to position themselves close to you.

Your first step in taking back your life and relationships is to identify those that will help you become successful. Listen don't try to think hard about this. Write the names of the people from page 28 that you said "deposit only."

My Current Relationship Circle

1.	
2.	
3.	
4.	
5.	
6.	
7.	
8.	
9.	
10.	

Identify Your Current Circle

Now that you have started, I would like to congratulate you for taking that all important step. Now that you have written the names of the people who currently make up your circle of relationships, it's now time to organize them.

Your Outer-Circle

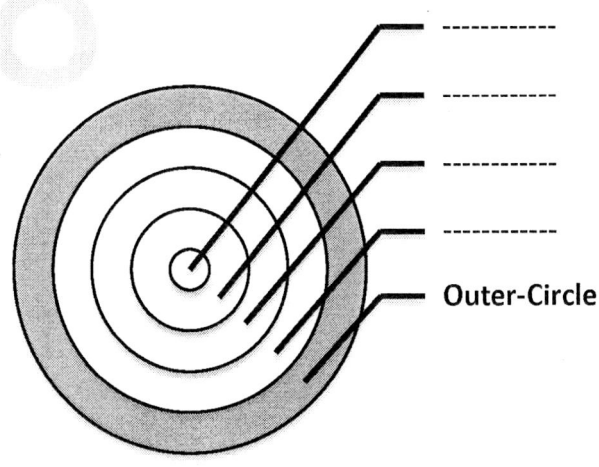

Outer-Circle

The first group or circle, of relationships is called your *outer-circle*. These people are those who you may have just met, and there is some type of common connection, professional or personal it doesn't matter. They don't have any personal information about you or your life except maybe your name and what you do. This is a very important level. It represents the outer gate of everyone's relationship circle. This is the place where everyone is free to roam without access into your true circles. If you are not careful you will allow someone access into a more privileged position then they should have. It is important to make people *graduate* into your more intimate circles.

In this circle, it is important to understand that knowledge is vital. If too much information is shared at this level, you risk violating your entire winners circle. Though transparency is popular, don't go telling your secrets to people you don't know. Each circle represents a level of worth and trust. Since communication is the vehicle that most people use to share information, at the outer-circle share as little information as possible. For example, when you meet someone on the street, the first thing you might say is, "Hello." You may give them your name, but not your phone number or personal information.

Healthy people would not tell you where they live or their social security number when they first meet you. This is purely a superficial circle. This is where you keep the relationship on the surface or at arm's length.

The relationships that you have are very important. You must *learn* how to protect those relationships and how to develop them. If you fail to do so, you will fail to grow and develop.

> *When you don't know how to use relationships properly you will abuse the relationships you have.*

The *outer-circle* is a very important level and where you will allow people to show their degree of respect and trust. If you allow people that you've just met to graduate to fast into your other circles, you may be putting your whole circle in jeopardy. Also I understand that this may be a tremendous amount of structure for you. However, I have learned that the easy road isn't always the best road in life.

People that you first meet must be proven before you allow them to advance into the more intimate spaces of your winners circle. Remember you must not give them too much information at this level. You should move as slow as possible in your outer circle relationships. Your best friend and biggest ally is your discernment. Feelings are important, but discernment is that deeper voice that most people hear but frequently ignore. There are definite signs into the true character of those who are in the outer circle. The *winners circle* will help master your ability to discern flaws and attributes within others.

The only information that you should give people in this introduction stage is things like your name, profession, and maybe some educational background. Also, at this level, you should learn how to master the art of *disposable talk* or superficial communication. You must try your best to keep outer court people at communication arms-length. Allow them to work their way through each circle appropriately. In this circle you don't absolutely know if they will be a part of your circle.

In the outer circle, there will be many people that may know your name and profession however this doesn't qualify them as experts on who you are. Also, you are not experts on them either. You may meet people throughout your life that you converse well with but they could never be a part of your *winners circle*. So be careful in this *filling-out-stage* not to say things like, "I feel like I have known you forever." Statements like that are commitment statements. Your feelings may be right and the conversation maybe good, but in all honesty, you don't know if you can trust this person yet.

The *outer-circle* of your relationships will always have more people hovering around, waiting to get more access into your more intimate spaces. You must understand your *self-worth* to manage your outer circle properly. In the beginning you may seem a little cold to people you have just met. Don't worry about that, they'll be okay.

You must take your time to build key relationships with people who will help you reach you potential. When utilized properly, your circle will establish trust, worth and value within your relationships. A vital key to the *winners circle* is, setting boundaries, and maintaining them.

Most of the trouble people encounter in relationships is a result of not maintaining boundaries. If you are able to maintain them, you will be able to improve yourself and those that are around you. Also remember that if you don't respect your boundaries, no one else will. Think about it, if you put your feet on the coffee table at your home, your guest will probably follow your lead and prop their feet up as well. Take your time to get to know people and slowly allow them to graduate into your important circles. You are a person of worth and value it's high time that you start acting like it.

What's under the mask?

Have you ever been to a costume party and everyone's dressed in weird outfits? Some people put an extensive amount of work into their costumes. Their hope is that no one will be able to guess who they really are. It seems fun and hilarious in the party setting, but the truth is, most people wake up to a costume bizarre every day. Millions of people have taken the time to disguise themselves before they walk out of their front door. They go to work, the gym, school, and restaurants with their mask and costume fully on, hoping no one will recognize the person underneath.

A costume party is done for fun and laughs but the life costumes are put on due to certain fears. Fear of people seeing the real person, the person that doesn't have all the answers, the person that feels weak and vulnerable most of the time, and the person that really don't know where they're going in life.

The Winners Circle

The *outer-circle* helps you take a peek at the eyes behind the mask of people you just met. Most people are very sensitive about their masks they can easily be defensive if you figure out the name of one or two of them. Yes, most people wear multiple masks. This shouldn't be a surprise to you because you probably are wearing a few yourself.

Just recently I met an old associate whom I went to high school with. We started talking, superficially of course. He and I were asking each other questions to find out if we still had the same interests. For the most part, we still had the same major-interests. For me, major interest is always a plus for future involvement. So, we casually hung out a few times, and talked a lot about our interests in ministry and family. However as time went on, he revealed that he wears a lying mask from time to time.

I viewed the new evidence as a teachable moment, and a way to build a closer bond. Not really to sit in judgment of him but to simply talk about that lying mask he had been wearing. You have to have hard conversations from time to time with people in your winners circle. However, he couldn't stomach the fact that his mask had been revealed, so he closed down and soon after the relationship was cut off.

The biggest lie you can tell yourself is that you don't wear masks. The best course of action is to identify what they are and deal with them. However, for most people, that is too much intimacy. So they would rather break the relationship connection with you and go on to someone who is less healthy about their relationships. I don't know about you, but there's no way I would let a liar hold an intimate position within my personal circle of relationships.

If you learn how to observe people and their actions, you will pick up on what they are really dealing with. This is not about *exposing* them but this is about *safety* and *right of passage*. If they are repentful and egger to change they deserve a second chance because no one is perfect. Everyone you engage with has some type of personal dysfunction they're dealing with. It's not your job to change them, but if they want to be a part of your circle, *you must decide what you'll put up with and for how long you will put up with it.* However let that be an informed decision, not a blind one. You need to ask the right questions in your outer-circle relationships. It is your right to choose who is a part of your life and relationship circle. Feel free to exercise your rights with bold righteousness.

This is where your boundaries meet personal masks. At this time, list the masks that you don't have the patience to deal with in your *outer-circle. A few instructions here this list shouldn't be long. Remember no one is perfect. Be as plain as possible about what type of personal dysfunctions you cannot tolerate.*

Outer-Circle: **Mask of Boundaries**

Example – Liar

1. _____
2. _____
3. _____
4. _____
5. _____

Remember what I said before. *If you don't respect your boundaries no one else will.* It is terribly important that you stick to the plan. If you see signs of these masks in people that are in your *outer-circle* or other circles, make sure you confront them right away. If you don't, it will only hurt you later on. After you become aware of their mask, find a non-threatening way to have an honest conversation about it.

A costume party is done for fun and laughs but the life costumes are put on due to certain fears.

Also, be smart. It is not required that you let dysfunctional people into your circle to help them. If you absolutely have to try fixing them, try helping from a safe relationship distance. However this isn't recommended in the beginning of building your *winners circle*. In all truth, I would strongly suggest that you refer them to someone else or just pray for them, but you will have to disconnect from them for a while. You need a strong circle with as many depositors as you can handle.

I don't believe that we can be all things to all people at all times. When you demand more from a person then they are able to provide, it causes an enormous amount of stress and pressure on your relationship. There are some people who will never change while having a relationship with you. I understand that maybe hard to grasp for fixers and caregivers. I'm not saying the person won't change, but they just won't do it while you are in their life. So be careful not to get hitched to people that could take too much out of you. That only slows your progress, and can make your life feel like you're treading through three foot-deep mud. In the end you will be left annoyed and frustrated.

Gone but not Forgotten

It's interesting when God kicked Adam and Eve out the Garden of Eden. Afterward, He placed an angel at its door to guard the boundary He had set. God sets the best example for us when dealing with people that have been repositioned or kicked out of our relationship circle. He put others that He trusted to guard the gate. Likewise you can use people within your circle to hold you accountable about others within and outside your circle. If they recognize that you have compromised your boundaries and let someone back in your life that don't belong, they then have the right to interrogate you about your decision. It isn't good for them to judge you but you should allow them to probe your reasoning.

I mentioned before that some people may not change their character while they are in a relationship with you. If you have to relocate or deny access to someone, it doesn't mean that you hate them. You are only saying to them, "We can't have a relationship at *this* time."

When God kicked Adam and Eve out of the Garden of Eden, He didn't forget about them. In fact, He began a plan of salvation to redeem them back into their rightful place. The only difference in the *winners circle* is that we aren't the redeemer. If you like, after someone has been denied access, you can wait for their change, but don't give them access into your *winners circles* until they can respect your circle and its integrity.

Now it's time for you to identify who's in your outer-circle. Take from the names you listed on page 80, and write whoever belongs in this relationship space.

The Winners Circle

MY Outer-Circle

1.
2.
3.
4.
5.
6.
7.

Your Associate-Circle

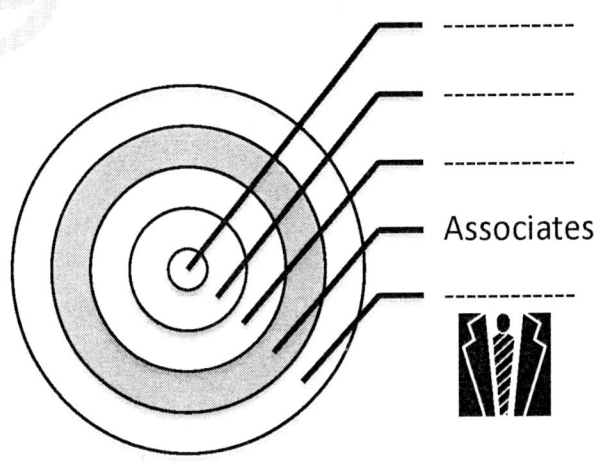

Associates

Associate - a person who shares actively in anything as a business, enterprise, or undertaking, partner, colleague, fellow worker.

Welcome to the second power level of relationship management. The associate level represents the first inner court of your tabernacle. This level is where certain people have the distinct opportunity to know more about you, your goals, and vision for life. Your associates are very important people. Those of you who are chasing dreams and are business minded may be familiar with the term "networking". Well, within your *winners circle,* networking is the best way to fish your outer court space for people who will become provision for your vision or dreams.

> *If you like, after someone has been denied access, you can wait for their change, but don't give them access into your winners circle until they can respect your circle and its integrity.*

It may not be wise to initially share your dreams with everyone, but you do need to share them with the right people. This is a little risky because you don't know if the person will laugh at you or take your ideas. This level is where the *risky business* takes place.

People that you work with on a day-to-day basis would probably be called associates. However, the people you should allow into this space are a little different. For example, I probably wouldn't invite most people at my job to my home for dinner, but there are a few that I would invite over. The ones that I would invite over would be good candidates for my associate level.

It is important in this space to share a little more of yourself. This doesn't mean you should disclose deep secrets, but it is okay to share your ideas and dreams with people you think might be sympathetic to them.

Who Do I Allow to Pass?

To control the traffic on our complex street systems, traffic control lights have been put in place by wise men and women. These lights give signals and direction to drivers whose paths intersect. There are some cars on these streets that are going in the same direction, and there are some cars that are moving in opposite directions. The next step in building your *winners circle* is to learn who gets the *green light* to move into another relationship circle. The people that get a green light are people moving in the same direction as you. The key is to find similar *interest.*

I used to believe that people who *value* the same things should get a green light. However, you will find out that you may have *similar values* with someone but *different interests.* Values are more stationary than interests. Interest can change and shift many times throughout a person's life. For example, I value God, my wife, and children. I live my life with those values at the root of whatever I do. Yet, I'm interested in non-denominational ministry, teaching people, sports etc... You get the picture.

My brother and I may value God, but if he is a sanctified denominationalist that hates sports, well, he wouldn't automatically get a green light into my *winners circle.* However, the priority here is to identify *your key-interests* and then look for those people who share them in your outer-circle.

Interests - Something that concerns, involves, draws the attention of, or arouses the curiosity of a person.

Values - Your personal constitution which governs your behavior and decision making.

You are looking for people that have common key interests in your associate level. You know the old saying "birds of a feather flock together". Especially if you are working on certain projects, you would look to give people green lights that could help you complete that project. Their value system may be somewhat different but they can still be a help on a particular project. You should at all times know why you let a person occupy a more intimate space within your *winners circle*. Make sure you have identified their key interests before you give them access into your associate circle.

Mentors

A mentor is one of the most powerful relationships that anyone can have in their life. There are two kinds of people who need a mentor. (1) If you come from a broken home or if you don't have strong connections with your immediate or extended family. (2) If you don't directly have a relationship with anyone that has done or is doing what you desire to do. The key here is *has done or is doing* what you are trying to accomplish.

Mentors are not only teachers but more so directors. Teachers may give you information while a director will show you the way around the piles of information and red tape. I am convinced that a good mentor is far greater than a college education. Though I'm an advocate of formal education, I believe how we are educated should be redefined.

I would pay Dr. I.V. Hilliard my entire college tuition to show me in four years what he knows about the ins and outs of ministry and business. There are some very successful people that had little to no education such as, Bill Gates, Russell Simmons, Harry Truman, and Walt Disney. The mentors who need to be a part of your associate level do not merely *have* potential they have already maximized their potential and have obtained the type of success you desire. They must have already tapped into their well of potential so that they can direct and teach you how to succeed in your particular area of interest.

> *Your winners circle will connect you with the people you need to be become the person you were designed by God to be. It will challenge the selfish individualistic model that has dominated the minds of so many Americans.*

The Bible teaches a very important lesson about people and relationships. Jesus asked a question, *"...Can the blind* lead the blind? Shall they not both fall into the ditch?" (Luke 6:39)KJ. The problem with most people's relationship circle is that they spend too much time with too many people on their level, and not enough time with people who are wiser than they are. The real issue here is pride. Pride is one of the biggest destroyers of success. It will stop you from listening to the hard things you need to hear.

If you could shut off the pride inside you and listen to a person that has *been-there-and-done-that,* you could get to where you want to be much faster in life. While other people are climbing ladders on the steps to success, you will be on the elevator going up to the top floor with your mentor.

Personal Numbers

Everyone has a personal number, and you should know the number of everyone that influences you. You must make sure you get people within your relationship circle that has a higher number than you. For example, if you are a five you must make sure that you have six and up in your *associate-level.*

There is no way you are going to reach your potential by spending five to ten hours a week around a group of fours and fives. That group may be a lot of fun and easy to relate too, but they can act as a huge stumbling block for you. If you ever desire to reach your potential and destiny, you cannot get there by constantly hanging out with peers and subordinates. The *winners circle* isn't all about work, work, work, either. You will be able to play and have fun, but that's what friends are for. Associates are not friends. I have to make that clear. Some associates may graduate into a friend, but everyone in your *associate level* isn't always permanent. Most of them may transition out of your circle over time. In Figure 1, you can see what a weak circle of relationships looks like. This is normal for people that are not focused on who revolves around them.

The Winners Circle

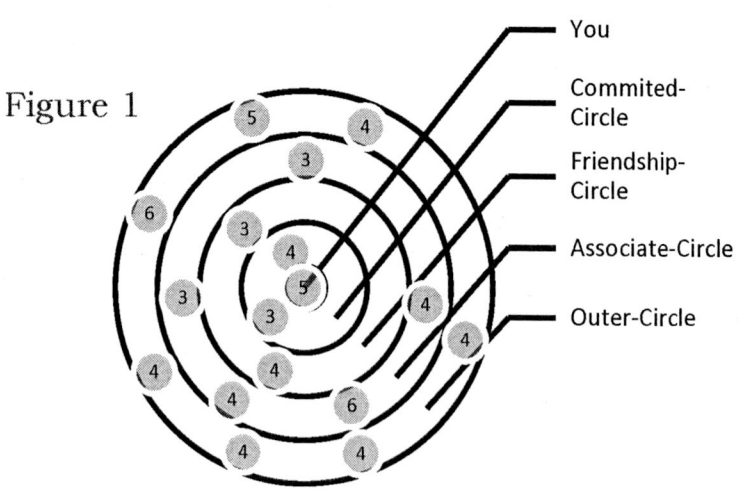

Figure 1

Your Associate Circle

You

Commited-Circle

Friendship-Circle

Associate-Circle

Outer-Circle

The numbers here represent people that you may engage with on a daily or weekly basis. These relationships could ultimately decide your ability and capacity. In Figure 1, the average circle number is four. Even though you may have a number slightly higher than those around you, it won't matter when the dominant personal number is lower than yours. In this case, the dominant personal number is four. Therefore, the number of the circle is four. What does this mean if you are a five caught in middle? It means that you will never achieve the dreams that you have with those people around you.

Personal Number Traits

1. Lacks appearance of good character, lies, cheats, manipulates, lacks spiritual grounding, completely selfish, have most likely accepted sinful/criminal behavior, do not have positive achievements.

2. Lacks appearance of good character, fear driven, easily influenced by others, when given the chance will exercise evil, selfish, confused about spirituality, lacks vision for life insight, resistant to authority, do not have real positive achievements.

3. Slight appearance of good character but only around family, may know their behavior is sinful, but enjoys those behaviors that are destructive, lust driven, gains strength from manipulating others, lacks positive vision for life, some education, little to no achievement.

4. Slight appearance of good character, weak to others, not a real threat to society, stuck between right and wrong behavior, idle, lacks vision for life, *may* have employment, possibly thinking about spirituality but not active in any ministry, little achievement (diploma or GED).

5. Appearance of good character, some spiritual understanding and slightly active in a ministry, inconsistent at best, may desire more for life, dealing with selfish ambition, spends time dreaming about what life could be like, may lack motivation, may fall for schemes, some achievement.

6. Appearance of good character, have accepted Christ as personal Saviour and active in ministry, understand God's call and vision for life, may lack capacity or experience, zealous, lack resources and support to fulfill divine vision, more achievement.

7. Kingdom builder, appearance of good character, spiritually grounded and

very active in ministry, understands God's call and has a definite vision for life, moving forward, having some success in completing vision, focused and is steadily gaining support, maintaining a *winners circle*, influences people, definite achiever.

8. Kingdom builder, appearance of good character, spiritually grounded and sold out to ministry work, lives a completely devoted life, has a definite vision and has achieved close to half of it, has good support, maintaining *winners circle*, influences many people, awesome achiever.

9. Master kingdom builder, appearance of good character, spiritually grounded and completely sold out to ministry work, spiritually mature, has achieved more than 75% of divine vision, and has mastered the *winners circle*.

10. Perfection - no one makes it here while in the physical body.

Make sure you seek out people who can be an asset to your winners circle. Sure, people on your level are comforting. People in your *winners circle* are there to challenge and push you at times. What you need is to spend time with people who are wiser and better connected than you are. When you spend time with your mentor, it's important that it is someone who you can be quiet and listen to. The number one reason why understanding is so absent in the lives of most people is because they want to be understood.

Remember, your mentors should have a higher relationship number than you. It's not your job to teach them anything directly, but you should listen to every word that comes out of their mouth. Also, remember that an associate wants cannot be all things to you. You should focus on learning from their strengths and disregarding their weaknesses. You may have someone that is terrific in business but has been divorced four times. They may be able to mentor you in business but when it comes to long term relationship advice, disregard every word.

I have different mentors who help me with various aspects of my life such as, family, ministry, and finances. For example, one of my mentors has been married for over 35 years. That is awesome to me and that is my vision for my marriage. So guess what our interactions are about? You guessed it: marriage and family.

> *The people that get a green light are people moving in the same direction as you. The key is to find similar interest.*

Remember, your winners circle isn't completely selfish. You should always desire to have a *win-win* situation in all your quality relationships. Therefore, after projects are completed, leave the relationship door open for those associates you have worked with. Give them the opportunity to use you at a later date. Make sure that you *owe no man but to love him,* even if your interest has completely changed.

Relationship Doors

This subject is important for many reasons. We all have relationship doors, but we all don't know how to identify and manage them. Mismanagement of relationships doors can quickly allow thorns to hurt your destiny and potential. After you start developing your *winners circle*, it is very important to assess and reassess your relationship circles. I would recommend every three months in the beginning.

As you make progress toward your goals and vision, you have to rearrange your associate relationships. Sometimes you will get attached to people you work with. Don't worry, it is a natural thing. However, it can be harmful over time when you both desire different directions. No one person in your *associate-level* will be all things to you. This is why you must relocate associates as your interests change. To do this, you should assess and reassess the key interests of those in your associate level at least every six months or so. Also, be careful of the soul-ties. Don't let someone take too much of you for too long. They may start acting as an anchor rather than an ore.

After a person has been relocated, you must decide what your future involvements with them will look like. This is where your relationship doors come in.

DOOR 1 – THE CLOSED DOOR

In life, you will learn not to burn bridges on your way up because you may need them on your way down. I believe that this saying has some truth to it. It's because of this saying that I try to do everything I can to make sure my relationships end in a good way. However, I have found that everyone in life doesn't share the same sentiment. There will be people you deal with in life and it will not matter what good you do to them, they won't take it well when you change directions.

Your Associate Circle

I had a good friend in college for four years that I was very close to. We shared a lot of good and bad times within those four years. Unfortunately, there was mostly bad than good. In about the third year of our friendship, I started desiring a different direction in life. I had changed a lot of my negative behaviors and interests. In that time we had a lot of awkward moments because we no longer had any key interests. He felt really betrayed that I changed. He got really upset when I would no longer go to the drinking parties or chase young ladies anymore. I tried my best to keep that relationship, but I later learned that I had to close the relationship door in order to continue making progress toward my personal goals.

What does it mean to close a relationship door? This simply means you deny access to a person that may desire to develop a relationship with you. You cut them off and lose their number. Most people will experience this in their life. However, closing relationship doors are only utilized as a last resort after someone has been hurt severely.

The *winners circle* will protect you from the wolves that will slowly pull you down into the land of bitterness and low self-esteem. Remember, this is first about safety. When an associate or anyone else within your circle began to depreciate the integrity of your vision, they must be relocated and sometimes DENIED ACCESS. When the relationship takes too much of you to keep and maintain it, do you have to tell the person that the relationship door has been closed? Yes and no. If you are good with words and can let someone know that it is better for the both of you to part ways, take the direct route. It is always better to let people know face to face. However, I know that way isn't always the choice of most people. So here are some ways you can send the message that you are not interested in continuing to invest in the relationship.

1. Don't answer their phone calls. Let it go to voice mail. Also don't return

email of any kind until it is totally convenient for you.

2. If they show up at your home unannounced, don't let him/her enter. Tell him/her that you are busy, and they should call before coming over.
3. When you do talk to him/her be really short with answers and responses. Use one word answers, yes or no.

Hopefully, they will get the message. Now I must warn you, this route is one of the weakest ways to close a relationship door. It is indirect and passive. Also it takes a lot of energy and time to pull off this process. My advice is to take the direct route even if you come off a little cold. You will get used to it after you have done it a few times.

DOOR 2 – THE REVOLVING DOOR

The revolving door is the best way to moderately give access to certain people. They have access into your life but it is limited. These are people who have worked with you on past ministry projects or other professional endeavors. After the work is complete, you might not have any more common interests, but the *winners circle* promotes a *win-win* situation. Even though the business is done, you must leave the relationship door open so that you can repay your debt. This doesn't mean that you have to call them every day, but it does mean that when you are called on by someone that has previously worked with you, you should be prompt in your response to them.

Do I have to say *yes* when an old associate call on me for help? It is very important to fulfill your debt to all your associates so I would advise you to do the *BEST* you can to be there for them. Your circle is about giving as well as receiving. Remember, you are trying to build bridges and maintain them. You have to try not to destroy them after you crossed them. However, you can't be there for everyone all at once. For example, suppose you are invited two events on the same date by two of your associates that you appreciate equally? What do you do? You must consider two things.

1. Who do you owe more?
2. Who called you first?

You have an obligation to those who have previously helped you. Therefore you are limited to a certain amount of associates you can manage at once. This is a major key in relationship management. Most people crowd their relationship circle with too many people. For some, it feels good to have a lot of people associated with them. One major problem with that type of relationship management is that you risk spreading yourself to thin. You must remember that you have to also help those that help and assist you. You can only take a limited amount of rain checks before someone realize that you don't value their relationship.

The associate level should have a limited amount of people within it. However it is not a set number of people. Everyone is different, and those differences need to be respected. Some of you will be able to have more associates, while others will only be able to manage five or so at one time.

DOOR 3 – THE OPEN DOOR

The open door isn't recommended in the associate level. It is one of the relationship doors that are commonly used by a lot of people but it shouldn't be extended to people in your outer-court or associate-level. The open door is given only to friends, family, and the one in your intimate circle.

Anyone who has an open door into your life has free access at all times. It simply means that they don't have to call before they come over. They just come over and some of them may have keys to your home and other important areas of your life. These are the people who can go into your refrigerator without asking your permission.

I have cousins that I don't see often but when we get together, they have the open door to ask me anything. The open door can be very dangerous when it is given to someone who needs a closed or revolving door. If you break an unhealthy relationship and close the relationship door, and that person shows up at your office or home unannounced, you should make sure they understand the relationship is closed, not open.

You must remember that you have to also help those that help and assist you. You can only take a limited amount of rain checks before someone realize that you don't value their relationship.

Now you can start building your associate circle. Remember, you need people who fit what you desire to do in life. Their skill set should compliment your purpose and direction. This is not about grabbing people out of the air, but you must enter it prayerfully and with patience. Your eyes will slowly open to the people you already have around you. You rub shoulders with some of the most powerful people on earth every day.

*Now it's time to identify your **Associate-Circle** and their main strengths, plus their personal number.*

1. Marcus Cage	Pastor/Spirit Counsel	6
2. Mary Top	Financial Advisor	7
3. Joe Graves	35yrs of Marriage	8
4. Phil Mark	Doctor/Health	6
5. Samantha Lap	Project Investor	7
6. Jessica Corey	20yrs in Business	7

~Next Page~

The Winners Circle

Your Associate Circle

1.		
2.		
3.		
4.		
5.		
6.		
7.		
8.		
9.		
10.		

Your Friendship-Circle

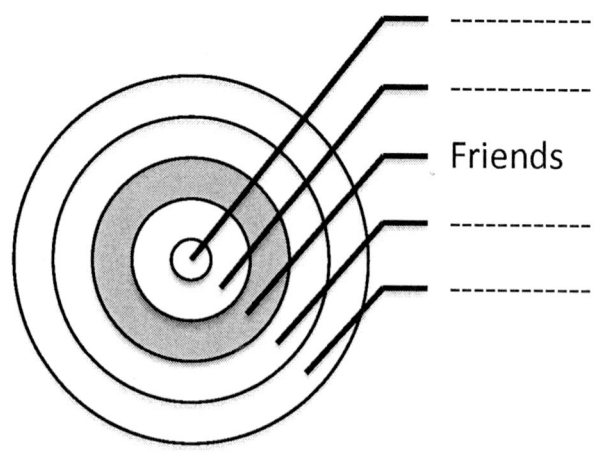

Friends

*A **friend** loves at all times...*

Proverbs 17:17

Most people that have lived past the age of thirty will agree that life is short. One of the best relationships that anyone will ever have is a friendship. I haven't had lots of friends in my life, but the few that I have, have been a permanent part of my life. In the all important *friendship circle* there are a few things to consider. (1) Small group vs. large group. (2) Choose your friends wisely. (3) Know your friends.

Small Group vs Large Group

It's funny to hear people boast that they have lots of friends. Most of the time, the number is much smaller than they truly realize. What has usually happened is that they confuse their associates as friends. However, when it's time to call on them for help or comfort, they won't be found because your so called friend won't share the same loyalties.

The question is, are smaller groups of friends better than larger groups? The *winners circle* is designed to help you figure out what you can handle. The truth is that it can be different for each person. However, I asked that you build one friend at a time. There is nowhere in the Bible that teaches that you should maintain many friends. While some might say there is some value in having many friends, it will get more difficult to be a friend to a larger group than a smaller group.

Every one of your friends put a demand on your time and energy. The more friends you have, the more time and energy you have to give away. In short, by having many friends, you are spreading yourself thin. Someone will be getting neglected in the long run.

A large group of friends would be five to ten people. Personally, I think that it is impossible, but I'm sure some people think they can maintain many friends. On the other hand, a small group of friends would be one to four people. Honestly, the best number of friends is three. Why? Λ small group of friends is the easiest to maintain.

Choose Your Friends Wisely

I know that you wouldn't seek out a friend as if the task was a part of your college homework assignment. Your friendship circle isn't as structured as the associate circle or outer circle. Developing your friendship circle has a more natural flow than the other circles. The truth is your friends are probably already a part of your life. Now what you need to do is carefully observe those that you know.

A good friendship is one of the best relationships you will ever have in this life. Yet the closer the relationship the more potential for great pain when things don't go the way they should. That's why you should choose your friends wisely.

Never rush into a friendship with anyone. Your friends should complement your character and ambitions. Also let friends graduate into their position in your life like every other person within your circle. You must learn how to make the good relationships in your life wait.

A lot of people fail miserably in their friendships because the expectations are too high. Your friends should have a personal number the same, one greater or one lower then what you have. This relationship isn't about direct teaching but more about transparency. It doesn't have an agenda and it can't always be on the schedule. A friend has an open door in and out of your life at all times.   Even if you haven't seen your friend for months, the moment you hook up, it's like you had been with them the whole time. True friends gravitate automatically toward each other like human magnets.

Though a friendship can provide many emotional, social, and other natural needs, the relationship isn't designed to solve all your problems. Again, a lot of people ask too much out of their friends. I found out as I grew older that although I love my few friends, my wife and children needs have to come first. When I was single and my friend called me, I would be there no questions asked. Yet after I got married, those late night hang out sessions had to come to an end.   That can upset people, even make them feel a little betrayed. Some of you may say that they were not a friend if they feel that way, but that is a very natural feeling, especially when you were bosom buddies and did everything together before the spouse.

Please don't make the people around you crazy by demanding too much from them. The Bible teaches us, "Do not trust a friend nor put confidence in a guide (*Micah 7:5*)." That means that there is only one being that can be all things to you and his name is Christ.

Know Your Friends

There is a verse in the Bible that teaches us to "know those that labor among you (*1Thess 3:5*)". This little piece of advice is priceless when it comes to dealing with people of all kinds. Specifically, it is important that you know those closest to you as well as possible. That means no surprises. Friends should mostly be predictable, that quality provides security and safety.

Too many surprises from a friend could put strain on the friendship. When you don't have any idea what's going to happen with the people around you, it can be a little nerve wracking. I had a friend in college that I knew was a little crazy or impulsive at times. If we went out and someone said a sarcastic comment, I knew that he would most likely respond with an even worst comment. So, in our friendship, I had to keep him cool most of the time. That got tiring quickly and it wasn't long before I learned that I can't be close friends with mad or angry people with no self-control.

Also, your friends should have similar if not the same key interests and values that you have. It's these key interests and values that will give your friendship longevity. As you age and mature, it is important that you mature together. A lot of friendships fail because people's key interests change over time, but values dictate friendships. Interest help friendships, but values are more important. Values are more foundational, and they are not easily changed. Make sure you take the time to find out if you and your friends have the same values such as, God, spouse, children, household, ministry etc... Though values don't change often in life, they can when your beliefs change.

What usually happens is that people try to hold on to a friendship though they know in their heart that their values have drastically changed. Remember we talked about soul ties. This is where we pick it up those unusual connections again. Relationships that you try to keep and maintain though you know you need to let them go will end up hurting you more than helping you. So to avoid any unnecessary hurt or pain, you may have to reposition your friend when your values change. Your relationship may have to be reduced to a few lunch dates a year or something along those lines. What you need to know is that it's okay if the friendship has to respect your growth and development. It should respect the lives and values of those involved.

There are some types of people who don't make good friends no matter what you do. I'm sure in your life time you have come across some difficult people. Some people just give off bad energy. I'm sure there is someone for everyone. As a rule of thumb, your friends shouldn't continually withdraw from you. When you're with them and after you leave them, you should feel encouraged and strengthened. If you usually feel frustrated, depressed, or annoyed after you leave the presence of your so called friend, it is highly possible that they are withdrawing from you. The best thing to do in that situation is to get a better friend.

There are some personalities that make for bad friends no matter what. Below is a list of these types of personalities that everyone should try to avoid when possible.

1. Angry personalities
2. Lying personalities
3. Strife-full personalities
4. Selfish personalities
5. Fearful personalities

It's not that these people won't have friends it's just that they can't maintain close relationships for a long length of time. Their personality deficit makes their relationships tremendously difficult. Besides, a friend should build, encourage, inspire, and strengthen your life. A friend makes your life richer. Now you have been given good tools that will help you identify your friends and manage those relationships. *In the friendship table list your friends, their personal number, and the years you have known them.*

Time to Build your *Friendship-Circle:*

Person	Person #	Years as Friend
1.		
2.		
3.		
4.		

Your Committed-Circle

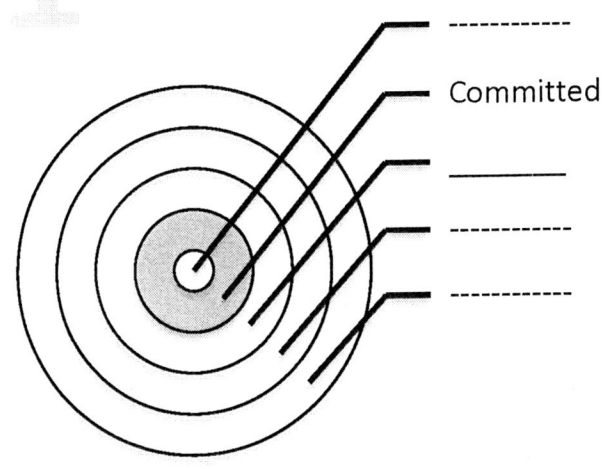

Committed

None but a mule denies his family.

Unknown

I used to wonder why we can't choose our families. It would make so many people happier if they could trade members of their family like NBA teams. If someone isn't doing what he or she should be doing you would *release* them from the family team. Also, you could make trades during the year. Every time a baby is born, they would all go into a family draft and we would take turns picking the ones we want. It would be great. All families would be built to win in life.

Okay, I know that sounds crazy, so let's get real. God is a master builder and I happen to trust that He knows what He is doing, even though we don't at times. Family is a beautiful system of connections and relationships.

The Importance of Family and the *Committed Circle*

Your family has played a very important part in the grand plan of developing you into the person you are today. I know some of you might say "they are why I have issues now." You may be right, but everyone has issues and dysfunctions. Even in the worst families a person can grow and develop into someone great. Some of the greatest people in the world came from dysfunctional families. With all the bad that can happen in families, a lot of good virtue can be realized and exercised.

When things are tough in life, the divine good that's in you rise to the surface. Of course, too much trouble can spoil even the most virtuous person. I just want you to understand that your family situation may not be all bad. They play an important role in your life. In your committed circle, you don't have to hang out with them 24/7, but from time to time you should find ways to engage with them. Face it, your close family knows you better than anyone in the world, and that's valuable.

Of course, there are some situations that may cause you to cut off certain family members. When there has been maltreatment such as:

1. Molestation
2. Abuse
3. Abandonment
4. Criminal Activity

You must act in wisdom even though you have the right to break a relationship if these acts have occurred against you. One of the greatest gifts you can give is the gift of

forgiveness. Though the pain of those actions can be great, over time you may want to pray about trying to forgive them who have hurt you. It will work wonders in your life and theirs. However, it is your choice. I know those scars can run deep.

On the other hand, you should not cut off your family for any other reason. On the next pages is a list of seven unjustifiable reasons that are common excuses for cutting off family members. When I say cut them off, I mean lose all contact with them.

1. Poor
2. Loud
3. Embarrassing
4. Uncultured
5. Uninteresting
6. Uneducated
7. Different States

Staying connected = Personal Grounding

There is an old saying, "blood is thicker than water". I'm not a scientist, but I would agree. Of course, what it means is that the connection or bond with your family is tighter than any other you may have in your life time. I'm reminded of Adam and Eve in the Garden of Eden. The Bible teaches that Adam and Eve stood naked before God and all creation. They had neither shame nor fear. It must have been a powerful state of life. Most people live their whole lives chasing this great state of freedom through all types of relationships. The truth is, those who know you the best have seen more of you, literally, psychologically, and socially.

One of the greatest gifts you can give is the gift of forgiveness.

The family that you grew up around has a special gift that no one else can give you: They know you best. That alone is a marvelous benefit. It should be respected and appreciated at all times.

What I'm saying is that it would be wise that you give your family some of your valuable time. Making family engagements and events have a way of grounding a person. If you can manage to stay grounded in life, when success comes it won't go to your head or spoil your heart.

Too many times I have seen people have a little success in life and cut all ties with their family members, only to find later that when the money, so-called friends, and temporary lovers are gone, they are left only with family. Some people remember that there is a place that has your name on it and it is called "home". If you can make it back there, you will be okay. There is a biblical story that shows this in detail, it is called, "The Prodigal Son".

Though you and your family members may have their differences, they are yours and you can't ever change that. You don't have to live next to your family members, but you should at least make time to see or call them every once in awhile. Below is a list of occasions that you should try your best to attend.

Family Occasions:

1. Graduations
2. Birthdays
3. Holidays
4. Special Dinners
5. Other Family Traditional Occasions

You should make it your business to stay in touch with family. Instead of making excuses not to stay in touch, try finding reasons why you can make it to those all important events.

Many people leave home to set their sights on saving the world, when it is more appropriate for your love to be shared at home and then abroad. Make sure you bring some of that caring and patience home to your family. In life it's important to maximize the relationships closest to you before venturing out to other relationships. Some of the best help and counsel in your life may come from your family members.

Now it's time to build your committed circle. Below, list the family members who you can promise to keep in touch with. Also put a star by the key family members who you can count on to be there for you.

Your Committed Circle

1.	2.
3.	4.
5.	6.
7.	8.
9.	10.
11.	12.
13.	14.
15.	16.
17.	18.
19.	20.

Your Intimate-Circle

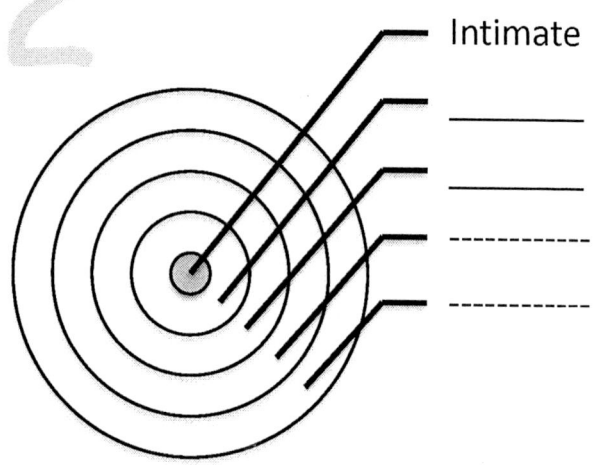

Intimate

Therefore shall a man leave his father and his mother, and shall cleave unto his wife: and they shall be one flesh. (Genesis 2:24)KJ

Welcome to the special space that exists within the *winners circle*. Unfortunately, today it is widely viewed as an optional space. Everyone might not have someone to share this intimate space with right away. It doesn't mean that you can't be fruitful or successful in life. Yet when this space is occupied by a wife or husband, the relationship has a way of making one's life very rich. If you don't have someone in your intimate circle, don't worry. This chapter can help you a little on how things should look when that time comes. It's always better to be prepared then not to be. If you have someone that you think may be a good fit for your intimate circle, this chapter will help you.

The Power of Two

You must continue to be careful about letting people graduate into these circles. Make sure that few people have toured your intimate circle. If you have had too many people in this space, it can slowly dilute its effectiveness within your winners circle. The more innocent the *intimate circle*, the stronger its integrity will be.

If you are the type of person who moves from one intimate relationship to another, you will not value this space the way it should be valued. This isn't just about sexual intimacy. If you learn how to nurture this relationship, it will nurture and cultivate you. However, if you have had lots of traffic in this space, there is still hope for you to make the intimate circle work for you.

All you have to do is sanctify the space. Within the spiritual world, this term is commonly used. It means to make it pure again or special. The American culture has slowly destroyed what makes the intimate relationship special. It has nurtured the idea of *free experience.*

If you want the best out of this space, sanctify it. Make it special to you and to the *one* that you share it with. For at least six months, don't have any intimate relationships or dates. If you can go longer, by all means do so. During this time, spend time with God as much as you can. Pray, read, write, go to church, participate in ministry or find a hobby. Use it as a time of personal rediscovery and spiritual development. While in your special time with God, ask Him to help you cut all the soul ties you have gained within other intimate relationships.

The *intimate circle* is a very important space. It works best within the *power of two.* Two are better than one, but only when two people walk in agreement. When you share this space with a spouse it can provide the strong push you need to *multiply your efforts.* It is amazing what an intimate partner can add to a vision.

When you have someone in this space consistently, it can be the backbone you need to give you the power to succeed. Relationships don't have to start as the best in this space, but it helps when it has steady growth and development. If there is no steady growth and development, it can block your success through domestic trauma. These traumas come in the form of divorce, heart break, constant fighting, and arguing.

There is no way a person can perform properly with continual domestic trauma. Therefore, it should be your ultimate goal to purposely nurture and pour love into this relationship. The intimate circle should be the first benefactor of your love and charity.

Years ago I realized that I would not make it to the mountain top alone, neither did I want to. What's even more powerful is that the Bible taught me that God's plan works best within the power-of-two. Surely Adam was special and complete before Eve was created, but she added a touch of uniqueness to the situation that he could never have added. God even gives the believer a degree of divine favor when this union is properly made. "A man that finds a wife finds a good thing and obtain *favor* from God" *(Proverb 18:22)NKJV*.

In short, it is in your best interest to make things work within the *intimate circle*. The more you start over, the more you devalue this space. This space can become desensitized very quickly. Many people that fail within the *intimate circle* settle for disposable, temporary relationships.

The All-In-One Space

Every space within the winners circle is special and unique. They each play a role that will help empower you to reach heights of success that may exceed your expectations. The *intimate circle* is hands-down the most unique and most powerful space within the winners circle. The reason for this is because it incorporates aspects and characteristics of all the other spaces except the outer circle. I call it the "the all-in-one space". The *intimate circle* represents the good in every other space within the circle. Keep in mind, its strength and power also makes it the most dangerous of all the other spaces. For this reason it should be not be taken lightly.

The *intimate circle* is the closet natural relationship that you will ever have on earth. I know some people may have other relationships they think are stronger, but that is out of order for your winners circle. The intimate relationship can be compared to the queen within the game of chess. It is the most powerful and versatile piece of the chessboard. The person within your intimate circle *will* be your closest associate, friend, and family member.

I know that sounds like a lot of hats to wear for one person, but that is one of the costs you must consider before letting someone into your intimate circle. If you noticed, I said the person *will be* your closest associate, friend, and family. You don't have a choice in this matter. Some people try and separate their romantic relationship from their business, only to find that it can't be done. Maybe your spouse doesn't go to work with you every day, but they can strongly impact your work life. The spouse is the biggest fan and supporter of every project and business decision. All relationships within your winners circle are connected to your purpose but at different degrees. You must learn how to value each relationship you have.

I have been married for eleven years. When God called me to pastor, it was not only a shock for me but it was one for my wife as well. At the time, she wasn't ready to be a pastor's wife. Her plans were closer to being a regular Sunday member. It was a huge vision change for our family. At first, I entered the situation with the understanding that God had called *me* to pastor and I have to fulfill MY assignment. Though there is some truth to that, it is wise to operate within the power of two. Agreement and cooperation is necessary when others will be affected by your decisions. I had to learn that the hard way.

I knew that two was better than one, but I thought that my obedience was all I needed to complete my assignment. I did, however, tell my wife that I was going to accept the call and move toward *my* purpose. I still didn't understand the power of agreement. I went ahead and founded Refuge Christian Center. In the beginning, I pushed and she pulled. At first, I took it personally and accused her of not loving me. There were times that she didn't want to go to church or participate in activities. I couldn't believe it. In every other church we were a part, she was very active and committed.

I almost had a break down trying to understand why she didn't want what I thought was the greatest job on earth. After about two years my pastor gave me the greatest piece of advice. He told me that my wife would greatly impact the success or failure of our church. The key for me was to realize that if I receive the call from God to do something that could drastically change the direction of our family, it is our family calling not an individual calling. So I set my heart to walk in agreement with my wife. That meant backing up. I was in full action mode while she was stuck contemplating that she was now the first lady of a spiritual community.

I envisioned us as a boat and I was the gas pedal and she was the anchor. I was fully committed and giving all the gas I could while my wife was stuck in the mud. That meant we were not moving toward our destiny. Unfortunately, a lot of married couples don't realize the power of agreement or the power of two. Only after a lot of wasted time and effort do they come to realize that these powers are keys to a healthy relationship. The odd thing about my wife was that she loved the ministry and the people, but she had not fully accepted any role within our spiritual community. That limited her commitment. I didn't know this because I didn't take the time to ask her what was going on.

Once we finally talked, I learned that she had been comparing herself to other first ladies she knew and felt like she couldn't be like them. She could not visualize any long-term role that would feel comfortable for her. After much prayer, patience, and joining Dr. Bridget E. Hilliard's First Ladies Network, she slowly gained passion for the youth and community outreach programming. We are now in full agreement and the ministry is growing like never before.

That is an example of the power of the intimate circle. Some people my say I'm already successful and I don't need anyone else. The power of agreement and the power of two with a spouse can double your success and anointing. Lastly, please don't minimize success to having money or material possessions. It is that and much more. There is a place in relationship bliss that no amount of money can buy. A good success means to be whole. You will need more than money to fulfill that. God bless you and I hope that you have enjoyed the *winners circle*. There is so much for you to do, so get up and start building your winners circle.

Go back to pages 80, 97, 124, and 135. Take the names from your list and finish the section on the next page.

The Winners Circle

Your Winners Circle

Outer-Circle

1.
2.
3.
4.
5.

Friendship-Circle

1.
2.
3.
4.

Committed-Circle

1.
2.
3.
4.
5.
6.
7.
8.

Associate-Circle

1.
2.
3.
4.
5.
6.
7.

Intimate-Circle

1.

Visit Us Soon

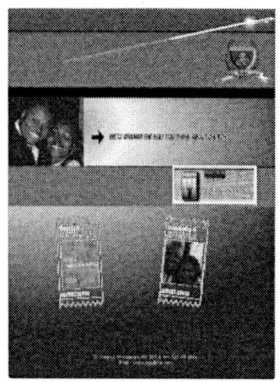

RCCMINISTRIES.NET

Check Out
Our Book Store

Coming Soon

Revised Edition
Rags To Righteousness

Don't Miss Out On

Refuge City

Christian Web Community

Lots of Fun

Meet New Friends

NetWork

Play Games

Blog Your Thoughts

Message Board/Forum

Photo Slide Shows

Contest "Win Money"

See You There!!!

Dedication

There are so many people who have played valuable roles in helping develop my soul. However, there is one special person I would like to give my deepest thanks and appreciations to, my wife and best friend. Thank You for always being there for me. I dedicate this work to you.

-Table of Content-